Fast Start Guide to Successful Marketing

For Books in the

Amazon Kindle Scout Program

By Diana Loera

Additional Books by Diana Loera

Pinterest Marketing for Authors and

FREE Bonus – Video Marketing for Authors

What I Did to Sell More Kindle Books on Amazon

What I Did to Sell More Kindle Books on Amazon Book 2

What I Did to Sell More Kindle Books on Amazon Book 3 Pay to Play

Fast Start Guide to Flea Market Selling

USA Based Wholesale Directory 2015

Best Venison Recipes

Party Time Chicken Wings Recipes and Bonus Dip Recipes

Summertime Sangria

And many more!

Table of Contents

Introduction

Hello! Diana Loera here.

I am a long time marketer – over 20 years in the direct response industry. I decided to follow my long- time dream of becoming an author and did so about four years ago.

As I began writing and selling my books, I realized that I did not have the marketing barriers or lack of sales that many authors experience.

I think my long time marketing career is what helped me easily clear marketing hurdles.

I then began writing books about my book marketing success and offering author services to help people gain marketing traction fast.

When the Kindle Scout program was unveiled I was quite intrigued.

This is an interesting program with a great reward for those who successfully complete the program.

I was contacted almost immediately by two authors regarding how to market and drive traffic to their Kindle scout nomination. I then realized that other authors may be able to benefit from my marketing insight if they were considering the Kindle Scout program.

With that thought in mind, I examined the program and created a plan that could be utilized over 30 days for fast marketing on a fairly short runway.

Marketing is a commitment. You can't just "wing it "or rely on the kindness of family and friends especially when it comes to the Kindle Scout program.

You will need to roll up your sleeves and be prepared to run hard for 30 days.

The good thing is, if you implement my marketing steps you will have a much easier time that someone with no marketing experience attempting to market.

The Kindle Scout program is somewhat like a beauty pageant. No matter how pretty you are – skill is a must have. We all know about the pageant parents – they are the ones who know the ropes and while their child may not be as pretty, she steals the show. Why? Because she has a seasoned team behind her. Now you will be assembling your team of marketing steps.

What is the Kindle Scout Program?

The Kindle Scout program is a new program that Amazon rolled out in 2014.

What makes it unique and different is that readers decide what gets published.

To give authors   a very basic overview -

Authors submit their books for consideration.

Readers vote on books and the winners of the voting round receive a publishing package from Amazon.

This is a very cool program but the million dollar question is – Is this the right program for you?

In this book, we will walk through details about the Kindle Scout program and as an established author, I will be offering my insight on the program from an author's perspective and also a marketer's perspective.

We will then cover marketing – including must do steps if you want the best chance of success and of being nominated a winner in the Kindle Scout program.

This is NOT a FREE MARKETING program. You will need to pay for marketing.

I receive a lot of emails every week from fellow authors asking about marketing.

I always ask authors what they are doing marketing -wise.

If an author replies – nothing or using the KDP free days (which is not marketing, by the way) or asks me what they can do free – I know that we have some work to do to get the author on track and to remove the rose colored glasses.

In this case – authors do not have access to the KDP program. They need to drive traffic to their book and get interaction from the traffic.

In this book we will be going over ways to drive traffic.

I do not recommend high priced programs nor do I promote affiliate links in my books.

I do recommend marketing that is consistent and affordable.

While every book is different and individual results may vary, the plan behind this book is to help you hit the ground running with your Kindle Scout promotion.

Benefits of the Scout Program for Readers

This program will appeal to readers who like to browse books that are at this point, not published. It will also appeal to readers who would like to get a free book.

To be successful, you need to attract readers who take the time to visit your book listing and then nominate your book for publication.

The way the Kindle Scout program is attracting readers is that each author must drive traffic to their book and get nominations. We will be discussing this in detail later in this book.

The book selection changes every 30 days.

Authors will need to do heavy marketing to build interest.

One smart move is that those who vote- if the book is published, the voter will receive a free e-book copy.

Your job as a participant is to get traffic to your book and get the traffic to interact.

A reader can nominate up to 3 books a month so if they manage to choose the 3 books that are published – they may receive up to 3 free books a month.

But many people will jump through flaming fire hoops for a chance to get something free. So with that being said – authors need to drive a large volume of traffic to help the odds of getting some interaction and ideally, clicks.

Authors who wish to participate must submit a never before published book for consideration.

Currently they are accepting English language only.

The current genres are as follows - : Romance, Mystery & Thriller, Science Fiction & Fantasy, and Literature & Fiction.

According to information provided by Amazon, Action & Adventure, Contemporary Fiction, and Historical Fiction will be accepted within the Literature & Fiction category.

Amazon recommends that you follow the Chicago Manual of Style.

You cannot be a co-author at this time. This program is currently for individual authors.

You need to be an adult (I am guessing 18 and older is what they consider to be an adult but if you are between 18-21 years of age, I suggest clarifying this requirement with Amazon).

You will need to provide a social security number or tax ID number and also have a bank account.

At this time, manuscripts should be about 50,000 words or more. Your book will need to be in a Word format. It should be ready to publish – in other words, checked for typos and properly formatted.

There are also requirements for your book cover. Suggested size provided by Amazon is a suggested 4500 pixels in height and 2820 pixels in width or a 1.5 height/width ratio).

Your cover must be in PNG (.png) or JPEG (.jpeg or .jpg) format and no larger than 5MB.

There is also an agreement that must be read and signed.

Amazon will review your application and decide if you will be in the next campaign or not.

If you're approved you'll receive an email notifying you of your approval.

You'll also receive a preview link to your book so you can see how your book will appear.

As all campaigns last 30 days, you'll be informed of the start date.

The more nominations that your book receives, the better the odds of being selected for publication.

Just because you make the first round doesn't mean your book will be chosen to be published.

This is just the beginning of the process. I highly suggest that you visit and review the actual site for this program.

The focus of this book is the marketing part needed but we are covering the basics of the Kindle scout program before we dig into the marketing so that you have basic info about the program at your fingertips.

If your book is approved you will need to have a marketing strategy in place.

If for some reason your book is not approved for the program you do have the opportunity to make changes and re-submit.

It will be up to you to let your friends, family, fans, fellow authors and the public know that your book is in the running for a possible publishing contract.

You will need to market- and market HARD.

Your book will need to receive nominations and a lot of them.

Your friends, family, fans and others need to follow a link that you will be given when accepted.

They will need to nominate your book.

You need to attract as many people as possible and this is where you need to really dig into marketing and marketing consistently for 30 days.

For 30 days you will need to market as hard as possible and understand that your competitors are doing the same.

This is a commitment and not for those who don't want to invest time and money into marketing.

So with all of this being said – are you ready to start working on your marketing strategy?

Marketing for the Kindle Scout Program

We will be creating a solid marketing plan to attract traffic.

The first step is to understand who can nominate your book – we need to target those who reside in the US.

The person will need a valid Amazon account.

Buying cheap traffic from freelance sites or other places is NOT going to help you. It won't help you now nor will it help you when your book is published.

Every week I receive numerous emails from authors who have tossed money into traffic promotions, Twitter promotions and Facebook promotions – in every single case, the author threw away money. While marketing is testing and measuring – we need to think and act before we pay for services.

We are going to cover various marketing options. I highly suggest that you do all of the options as you need to build a high volume of awareness fast.

Following are several steps, outlined one by one, to help you to create a solid marketing platform as quickly as possible.

While they are listed as options – I strongly recommend that you implement all of the options. This is not the time to penny pinch or cut corners.

Marketing Option Number 1

Linked In

Linked In is a business-oriented social networking service. Founded in December 2002 and launched on May 5, 2003 it is mainly used for professional networking.

Just to give you a fast overview regarding the number of people on Linked In and potential for people to see your marketing promo -

In 2006, Linked In was at 20 million members. I joined Linked In around 2004 and really began working it around 2008.

In June 2013, LinkedIn reported more than 259 million acquired users in more than 200 countries and territories.

The site is available in 20 languages, including Chinese, English, French, German, Italian, Portuguese, Spanish, Dutch, Swedish, Danish, Romanian, Russian, Turkish, Japanese, Czech, Polish, Korean, Indonesian, Malay, and Tagalog.

In July 2013, Linked In had 65.6 million monthly unique U.S. visitors and 178.4 million globally. By October of the same year, it had increased to 184 million.

LinkedIn now has more than 300 million members in over 200 countries and territories.

It is significantly ahead of its competitors Viadeo (50 million) and XING (10 million).

The membership grows by approximately two new members every second.

With 20 million users, India has the fastest-growing network of users as of 2013

Linked In is free to join and I hope that it is already a platform tha you're using.

I built my Linked In account over the years and now have over 29,000 contacts.

If you are not on Linked In yet – today, make it a must do project to sign up.

Ideally, you're already using Linked In. There are numerous author groups as well as a wealth of other groups where you can post information about your book.

Like with any other social media platform, you don't want to be doing a me, me, me every time that you post.

You do need to build rapport and interact with others on a regular basis.

NEVER send a mass message to all your Linked In contacts – this is frowned upon and highly irritates people.

Instead – simply post in the updates regarding your participation in the Kindle Scout program. Include a link and ask for a nomination. You may want to mention that those who nominate you will receive a free copy when you win.

If you are in groups, you may be able to find the opportunity to promote your book and ask for votes.

Just do not get in a hurry and sound like a spam machine. While you have a deadline, you also need to market properly.

If you send an email to me via loerapublishing@hotmail.com I will send a promo out to my contacts regarding your book.

If you need help crafting your message to send out to your contacts – the above email address will bring you to me.

Marketing Option Number 2

Pinterest

With 70 million users world-wise, Pinterest is the fastest growing social media platform.

Pinterest users are proven to convert into buyers at a higher percentage than Twitter or Facebook. That is not to say- don't use Facebook or Twitter but know how to maximize viewers by using the work horses of social media – Linked In and Pinterest – to your advantage.

If you do not already have an established Pinterest board – you are missing one of the hottest opportunities available for authors.

You need to create and maintain a Pinterest account- or have someone do it for you. I never said that this was going to be an easy path and in your case – you will need to hustle.

This is a link to my Pinterest board www.Pinterest.com/Loera

Please feel free to follow me and I will follow you back.

If you send a link to me of your pin promoting your book on Kindle Scout, I will ask my assistant to pin it on my Kindle Scout Pinterest board – FREE at no expense to you.

If you have a VA – virtual assistant – you can utilize them to do a lot of the daily promos for you. If you don't have an assistant yet, set your mind to making one solid hour a day – promo time.

Pinterest is a top book sales platform for me. You can use it to drive traffic to your Kindle Scout book and later when your book is published, use it to drive traffic and sales.

Marketing Option Number 3

Twitter

Twitter is a valuable part of book marketing.

The challenge is once again you don't want to saturate your followers with a me, me, me flood of tweets all about voting for your book.

You also don't want to buy junk promotions – these are usually offered by people who prey on others – their account or in many cases multiple accounts – are filled with fake users.

No one is reading your message if you are paying to have your tweet placed on sites with huge amounts of followers yet no activity or retweets.

You need to ensure you are interacting with Twitter followers who are real and who read and ideally, retweet.

It is better to tweet to 10,000 people and receive 35 retweets than to promote to 100,000 fake or non- active followers and receive nothing.

You need to build rapport with your followers and retweet consistently.

I do not recommend auto retweet programs as you may find yourself in hot water after retweeting something that you don't agree with or that is spammy.

I use HootSuite, actually my assistant does, to stagger out tweets throughout the day. We just signed on for a free 30 day trial of the Pro version which is currently 14.99 a month.

As of now, we have not seen the value of the Pro version and experienced numerous snags and problems.

With that being said, once we are past the learning curve, if we are still experiencing challenges, we will go back to the free version.

You may want to check out Hootsuite to see if it may of value to you as far as scheduling your tweets. Look at the free version and give it a try if it interests you.

Marketing Option Number 4

Video Book Reviews

You may be thinking to yourself that your book isn't published yet so this option isn't applicable.

It is an important part of driving people to vote for your book.

You can create a video of yourself encouraging people to vote for your book.

However, I suggest utilizing someone who has the right equipment and knows how to craft a video review.

Points to cover –

Details about your book

Building excitement about the nomination

How to vote

Details regarding how the voter may receive a free copy of your book

A very solid CTA – Call to Action – driving the person to act now

If you need resources for a video book review – contact me via email and I will share my current resources with you. I have found that for some reason, people who produce the video book reviews often stop or take time off.

Therefore, I don't want to list people only to have you discover they are no longer accepting clients.

Marketing Option Number 5

I highly advise contacting your local library. Ask if they have reading groups and/or groups for writers. Ask if you can speak to the groups about your Kindle Scout nomination.

If you have a local bookstore, call and ask if they have reading groups and author groups. Schedule time to present your motivational story.

I advise taking a handout with your url and instructions on it. Be prepared to answer questions others may have regarding participation in the Kindle Scout program. Remember – you are now the expert as you are in the trenches – you've gotten yourself into the nominated books. You have valuable info to share with others.

Try to time it that you receive coverage from your local TV, radio and newspaper media. Having this coverage before presenting at bookstores and/or the library as this then provides extra credibility.

Marketing Recap

After reading the marketing options just mentioned, you may be thinking that this isn't anything new or anything that you don't already know.

Interestingly enough, most authors do not use the previously mentioned options or do so sporadically.

Instead many do what I call throwing spaghetti on the wall – randomly trying this and that with no focus and often a lot of money spent. The end result is an empty wallet and no payoff.

My success list is rather simple –marketing doesn't need to be complicated. The main thing is to be organized, consistent and adhere to a plan.

The options listed are proven drivers of traffic but that traffic will not arrive if you do not do your part.

You need to commit to spending a minimum of a solid hour 7 days a week promoting your book – be it a Kindle Scout nominated book or a published book. Marketing is the key to driving sales.

Repetition goes hand in hand with marketing.

Repetition

Repetition is a must do with marketing. Never think that because you did one pin, one tweet or one Linked In promo that millions are reading and responding.

You need to build a consistent pattern each day and each week.

One recent non- author marketing program that is a great example – My husband owns a lawn care business. We hire high school kids to deliver flyers in the spring.

Last week, one teenager commented to me that we had placed flyers in the neighborhood that I was sending him back to and he had just been there the week before.

The Monday after delivering the flyers, my husband's company received 10 calls – every single person had received a flyer the week before on that block.

The first week he received two phone calls. This is a 20 home block. The windfall of 10 was generated through – yes, you know it – repetition.

This is the exact same with ANY type of marketing – be it books, lawn care, insurance, tire sales or whatever. So many people give up after the first marketing round as they do not understand repetition is needed.

In the case of author marketing – we need to establish repetition. We test and measure our copy. We see which copy generates the most sales.

Does the response increase the third week or fourth week?

What words in our copy entices the best reaction?

Money Wasters

While marketing does need testing and measuring so one can determine the successful actions and repeat them – there are money wasters that one needs to avoid.

I know I have mentioned money wasters before in this book but their siren song is so tempting, I know it is hard to resist.

In your mind you may be thinking but this offer is different – it isn't a money waster.

Any phony driving of votes from various accounts is just not smart.

Any promises that seem to good to be true most likely are money wasters.

As we discussed earlier in this book, people who are tweeting to large accounts – or even smaller ones – need to have real followers and people who retweet.

I suggest looking at the retweets on the Twitter account before deciding to purchase tweets.

I will give you a stellar example of an account that gets retweets like crazy.

William Potter is the founder of the Independent Author Network. When your book is published, I highly suggest joining his network for authors.

But along with the Independent Author Network, he offers a Twitter service – very affordably and the authors retweet like mad. If you visit www.AuthorTweetService.com you will find several Twitter promo options – all very affordable.

They also react to tweets.

William is one of my top marketing resources because he is a sincerely good person and he runs an ethical business.

I don't take any kickbacks for mentioning him and he will probably be a bit embarrassed when he finds out that I am crowing about his network but I think as authors, we need to find and share stellar resources with each other.

Independent Author Network is one that I highly recommend and when you compare them to others you will quickly be able to weed out money wasters as William runs a class act program.

Making the Cut – What Happens When Your Book is Selected

If you are selected, you will receive an email notification from the Kindle Scout program notifying that you have won.

Currently, you then have 30 days to do the following steps-

Submit your final manuscript

Submit your final book cover image

Submit your banking information

Submit your tax information

Remove your entire book from ANY sites where your book is being offered for free. You are currently allowed to keep a snippet of up to 10 percent of your book posted online for marketing purposes.

Once ALL of the above is done, your book will be made available to browsers on Amazon.

One week before your book is made available for sale, all of the people who nominated your book will receive a free copy.

I suggest that you have everything needed above ready to go by the second week of your marketing campaign.

If you are posting your book as Free – make sure you find out beforehand how to remove it online and how long it takes to be removed as that is the area that I see causing the longest hold up.

Advances and Payments

Of course, once you are selected, you will want to know how soon your advance will be sent.

Your advance delivery hinges on how fast you can get the list we just covered done.

All of the paperwork needs to be done correctly.

Your final manuscript and book cover will need to be in house and approved. Note the word – approved.

Once everything is in house and approved, the current advance time is within thirty days.

Just like with the royalties that I (and other authors) receive from Amazon and Kindle, you will be paid monthly by Kindle Press.

The first few times I was paid, I only checked my softcover royalties and then I discovered my e-book royalties were even larger! I remember that first feeling of excitement and still am excited to check my royalties monthly. It gives me an immense satisfaction to see my work pay off into a book that people buy and enjoy and a nice compensation for me.

You will see your royalty statement posted in your Author Central account about thirty days after the end of the month in which sales happen.

Kindle Press may decide to hold your payment until you reach a certain amount. The amount is currently 50.00. Don't worry though if it takes you a month extra to reach the first 50.00. The fact is you won and you made it through the first hurdle.

Now you need to focus on selling as many copies of your book as possible. You may want to write and release a press release regarding your winning book. Contact your local media – TV, newspaper and radio station and get your publicity moving.

Please email me and I will send out some promos to my contacts about your winning success.

I wish you the very best with your Kindle Scout marketing and hope to see you with a winning book.

Marketing of Winning Books

Winning books will be enrolled in and earn royalties for participation in the KOLL -Kindle Owners' Lending Library - and Kindle Unlimited.

Winners will be eligible for targeted email campaigns and promotions but the frequency has not been announced. Plus notice the word eligible – it doesn't state that they will do your marketing for you.

Being blunt- you still need to market your book.

Once your book is published you should send out press releases and follow a marketing strategy using social media platforms.

My top favorites are Linked In and Pinterest but I do suggest adding in Twitter also. Video book reviews and book trailers are a must do too.

As we also discussed – contact your local media. Create a buzz about your book and watch the sales start to roll in.

Closing

With the above being said, I'm going to wrap up this book now. I appreciate that you bought my book.

You have a very exciting opportunity ahead of you with the Kindle Scout program.

I do hope that you email me and update me on your marketing as you progress.

Writing books takes time, energy and focus. Marketing also takes the same time, energy and focus.

I have been able to create a good revenue flow by writing books and I hope to see your name in the author ranks soon.

You CAN do it. Don't let anyone sway you from your dream of being a published author.

Sincerely,

Diana

www.ingramcontent.com/pod-product-compliance
Lightning Source LLC
Chambersburg PA
CBHW051349290326
41933CB00042B/3352